Copyright © 2025
Janet Groom
Twinkle the Sleeptime Unicorn
Bedtime Stories

ISBN: 978-1-917779-29-6 (paperback)
ISBN: 978-1-917779-30-2 (ebook)

First Edition
Published by ALP House Publishing
www.alphousepublishing.com

ALP HOUSE
PUBLISHING

* * *

All rights reserved.

No part of this book may be reproduced by any mechanical, photographic or electronic process, or in the form of a phonographic recording, nor may it be stored in a retrieval system, transmitted or otherwise be copied for public or private use, without prior written permission of the author/publishers.

* * *

Cover Artwork created by Groom Graphics using Canva Pro

THIS BOOK BELONGS TO:

_____

HELLO LITTLE DREAMER, I'M TWINKLE

I HELP CHILDREN, JUST LIKE YOU,
TO FALL ASLEEP,
SO WE CAN FLY TOGETHER TO
THE LAND OF DREAMS

♥

Twinkle's Nighttime Ride

When night stars
softly sparkle and gleam,
Twinkle the Unicorn
rides through your dream.

With a shimmer of stardust
and wings full of grace,
She carries you off
to a magical dream place.

In a starry night sky, high above the clouds, lives a gentle unicorn named

TWINKLE

TWINKLE HAS A SHIMMERING RAINBOW MANE, SPARKLY HOOVES, AND A HORN THAT GLOWS WITH SLEEP MAGIC.

Every night, when the moon rises high in the night sky, TWINKLE flies down on a rainbow path to visit babies and young children.

TWINKLE'S JOB IS TO HELP
YOUNG CHILDREN AND BABIES
TO CLOSE THEIR EYES
AND DRIFT
INTO A LAND FILLED WITH
SWEET DREAMS.

SHE SPRINKLES
HER RAINBOW DREAM DUST
FROM HER HORN
AND SINGS
A LULLABY SO SOFT AND SWEET.

One evening, TWINKLE visits a cosy bedroom where a sleepy child snuggles with a soft, fluffy teddy bear.

The child is tossing and turning, unable to sleep.

TWINKLE
GENTLY WHISPERS,

"SHHH, MY LITTLE ONE.
IT'S TIME TO REST
AND DREAM."

WITH A SWIRL OF DREAM DUST, THE CHILD BEGINS TO SMILE AND YAWN.

THEN, A RAINBOW BRIDGE APPEARS, AND THE SLEEPY CHILD FLOATS THROUGH THE COLOURFUL DREAM CLOUDS WITH TWINKLE.

TOGETHER THEY SOAR THROUGH THE SKY,
PAST TWINKLING STARS
AND A SMILING MOONBEAM.

IN MOMENTS, THEY REACH
THE LAND OF DREAMS

A MAGICAL PLACE WHERE
TEDDY BEARS DANCE
ON DREAM CLOUDS.

AND GIGGLING STARS
PLAY PEEKABOO
IN MEADOWS OF
TICKLING FLOWERS.

TWINKLE LEADS THE SLEEPY CHILD
TO A MAGICAL BED
MADE OF DREAM CLOUDS
AND
SWEET LULLABIES.

"Rest here, sweet one," whispers TWINKLE, "and dream the happiest dreams."

As the sleepy child snuggles into the fluffy bed, TWINKLE lies down and her unicorn horn glows with sleep magic.

"Goodnight, my little dreamer," she whispers, "sweet magical dreams."

AND WITH A YAWN,
THE CHILD FALLS ASLEEP,
DREAMING OF LOVE,
GIGGLING STARS
AND
DANCING TEDDY BEARS.

Twinkle's Sleeptime Affirmation

I am calm,
I am safe,
I am loved.
With Twinkle by my side,
I drift into sweet dreams
and magical adventures.

Twinkle's Special Sleeptime Poem

Close your eyes, my sleepy star,
Feel how calm and still you are.
Take a breath, soft as the breeze,
Floating gently through the trees.

Your eyelids are heavy, now your nose,
A sleepy wave from head to toes.
Your hands relax, your eyes close tight,
As stars above shine soft and bright.

Imagine now a glowing light,
A magic cloud so fluffy white.
It lifts you up into the skies,
Where dreams begin and worries fly.

You're safe, you're loved, you're wrapped in peace,
As nighttime brings a sweet release.
Drift and float in dreamland deep,
It's time for rest... it's time for sleep.

TWINKLE SAYS IT'S TIME FOR SLEEP

NIGHT, NIGHT AND SWEET DREAMS!

More Children's Stories & Books...

Author, Poet & Indie Publisher
www.janetgroom.com

www.janetgroom.com/childrens-books

Etsy
SoulMagicInspiration
Kids Books and Gifts to Inspire and Promote Kindness

Herne Bay, England

www.etsy.com/shop/SoulMagicInspiration

www.ingramcontent.com/pod-product-compliance
Lightning Source LLC
LaVergne TN
LVHW071652060526
838200LV00029B/444